Contents

How has travel changed?   6

Short journeys   8

Horse-drawn transport   10

Cars   12

Roads   14

Traffic controls   16

Buses and trams   18

Barges   20

Trains   22

Ships   24

Flying   26

Glossary   28

Further information   29

Index   30

How has travel changed?

People could travel on the sea, by road and by rail early in the twentieth century, just like we do today, but the transport we use has changed in many ways.

1930

Now

This picture shows local **traders** in 1930 transporting their loads by horse and cart over Tower Bridge in London. Journeys in a horse and cart could be very slow.

Lorries like this one on Tower Bridge today can carry much bigger loads longer distances.

Changes in **technology** over time have improved transport in many ways. The invention of the motor car at the end of the nineteenth century changed road travel forever. Travelling by road became so much quicker and easier.

In the air meanwhile, the **jet engine** allows planes to take people quickly to anywhere in the world.

Short journeys

There were few cars around in 1900. People had to find other ways to travel to work or to the shops. Short journeys were made on foot or by bicycle.

The bicycle was the first form of wheeled transport that ordinary people could afford. Families from the town often enjoyed cycling out into the fresh air of the countryside.

1890

Look at these old bicycles from 1890. They had no gears and just one brake. Imagine riding up a hill without gears!

Do you think it would be comfortable riding a bicycle in a long skirt?

Look at this modern bike. How is it different to the old bicycles on the opposite page? In what ways is it similar?

Bicycles are more comfortable and safer than they were in the past. Gears make cycling less tiring. Brakes at the front and back make stopping easier.

Although we now have cars, many people still walk and cycle about. In towns cycling can be quicker than driving if the roads are busy.

How are these cyclists keeping safe?

Horse-drawn transport

People have used horses for transport for thousands of years. Around a hundred years ago this type of travel was still very common on the roads. Horses and carts were used for transporting heavy loads.

1910

Wealthy people often travelled in their own horse-drawn carriage. This picture shows people hiring a horse-drawn carriage called a **hansom cab** in 1910. This was like hiring a taxi today.

Do you think these people were rich or poor? Why?

Horses are not used for travel very much now. Motor **vehicles** have replaced horses and horse-drawn transport on the roads.

Some people do still ride horses but usually this is just for fun.

Bridleway: walkers, horse riders & cyclists only

Hampshire County Council Countryside Service

This photo shows horse riders on a bridleway. A bridleway is a track for horses.

Cars

From the 1940s many more families could afford to buy a car. It changed the way people lived. They could get around much more easily.

1946

The photo shows a **parade** of new cars for sale in 1946. All of the cars are a similar shape and colour. They had long bonnets and shiny **chrome** bumpers. Most cars were painted in black or another dark colour. Many of them had no windscreen wipers, seatbelts, heaters or **indicators**.

Today's cars are a lot more comfortable. The seats are nice and soft. In the winter you can turn on the heaters. They are also a lot safer. Every car has seatbelts. Many have airbags.

Cars now come in a lot more different shapes and colours.

Look at the cars in this photo. How do they look different to each other?

Roads

Main roads were narrower in the past than they are today. The road surfaces could be very bumpy and rough, too. They got rutted by the heavy iron wheels of the carts and carriages.

1920

The narrow road in this picture was in fact the main road between Stoke-on-Trent and Stafford.

Nowadays there are far more vehicles on the road. Main roads have to be safer and wider.

The main road between Stoke-on-Trent and Stafford is now a **dual carriageway**. It can hold two lanes of traffic in each direction. The **central reservation** stands where the trees used to be.

Now

What has been built to help people cross the dual carriageway?

Motorways like this one have several lanes of traffic. You still get jams though!

15

Traffic controls

Travelling through a crowded city centre with your car or horse and cart a hundred years ago could be difficult.

1912

Look at this 1912 photograph of Piccadilly Circus in London. There were no road lanes, traffic lights or signs to control the traffic. Accidents were common.

The road layout in Piccadilly Circus has changed a lot since 1912. In 1926 traffic lights were placed here for the first time.

Now

Then and now

Look at the traffic there today. It runs a lot more smoothly. There are rules in place for drivers. Do you know what the yellow boxes on the road are for?

Look at the famous statue of Eros in this photo. In 1912 it was in a different place. Can you find it?

Buses and trams

Eighty years ago most big towns had buses, but many also had a tram service. Trams like this one in Nottingham drove down the middle of the road on metal tracks.

1928

Trams were powered by electricity from overhead wires. The tram tracks in most towns were dug up or covered over in the late 1940s. The motor bus was seen as a better method of transport because it did not need rails.

What is the motorcyclist in the corner of the picture wearing on his head? What do motorcyclists wear today?

Trams are less common in British towns today although some towns like Nottingham are laying new tramways.

Buses are the form of **public transport** found in most towns and cities today. This street in London is only open to buses, taxis and bicycles.

Buses and trams have their own lanes in most busy cities.

Do you think it is better to use a bus or tram in town rather than a car? Make a list of your reasons.

Barges

Transporting very heavy goods long distances by road was not the best way a hundred years ago. The roads were rutted and muddy, and a horse and cart could not hold large and heavy loads.

1908

It was easier to transport very heavy goods by train or by barge on a river or canal. The barges were pulled along by horses on a **towpath**.

How is the **cargo** being unloaded on to this barge?

Canals are rarely used for transport now. Many old barges have been converted into comfortable homes for people to live in.

Can you see the old towpath on this picture?

Now

You can hire a barge for the week and spend your holiday travelling around and living on the canals.

Trains

1963

By 1850 railways had been built across much of Britain. For the next hundred years trains were the main way that people and goods travelled around the country.

Trains in the past were powered by steam engines that burned coal. These trains were used until the 1960s. Look at the train above in Ludlow train station. Steam trains belched out smoke and steam.

1963

Now

Taking the train is still a popular way to travel. Look at the modern train in Ludlow station today. Trains now run on **diesel** fuel or electricity. They make less noise and don't make the air so dirty.

Then and now

Look at the photos of Ludlow station in 1963 and today. The old building has been knocked down and replaced by a smaller station. Which do you like best?

Now

Ships

If you could afford to travel abroad a hundred years ago you went by steamship. Trips over the ocean could take days or weeks to complete.

For ordinary people travel by ship was uncomfortable. They stayed in small cabins low down in the ship.

1889

1932

For the rich the trip was more glamorous. They had luxurious rooms and fine food. These first-class passengers are enjoying themselves on deck by the pool

We still use ferries to make short trips across the sea. But if people go far today they usually fly by plane. People now only take long journeys on a ship for pleasure. This is known as a **cruise**.

Cruise ships have entertainment on board such as a theatre and swimming pools. Luxury sea travel is no longer only for the rich.

Now

Find out for yourself

What famous ocean liner struck an iceberg and sank in 1912?

Flying

Travelling by aeroplane was very rare in the 1930s. Look at the picture of this **propeller**-driven plane from 1934.

1934

The plane was much slower than the jet aircraft we fly in today. It was also much smaller. This plane could only carry around 40 passengers. An airport then was often just a small field.

Long-distance travel is more common today and people use aeroplanes more than ever. Flights are much quicker and cheaper than they used to be.

Modern jet-powered aeroplanes can carry hundreds of passengers. Aeroplanes now take off and land at large airports like this one.

Jumbo jets

The Airbus A380 is the largest passenger airliner in the world. It can hold over 850 passengers and started flights in late 2007. Its nickname is 'Superjumbo'.

Glossary

Cargo Goods carried by ship, barge or aircraft.

Central reservation The strip of land between the carriageways of a major road.

Chrome A decorative or protective coating made from the metal chromium. It is often used on motor vehicle parts.

Cruise A holiday on a ship that stops off at several places on the way.

Diesel A type of fuel that is often used in large vehicles such as buses, lorries and trains. It is used in some cars as well.

Dual carriageway A road with a strip of land dividing the traffic travelling in opposite directions.

Hansom cab A type of horse-drawn carriage that could be hired. The driver sat behind the cab which seated two people.

Indicators Flashing lights on the sides of a car to show which way a driver is turning.

Jet engine An engine that creates the forward thrust needed to move an aircraft. It works by burning a mixture of air and fuel inside the engine and then forcing it out of a small opening at the rear.

Parade Moving show of vehicles in a group.

Propeller One of a set of spinning blades that provide the force to move a vehicle through the air or water.

Public transport Transport such as buses or trams which run on fixed routes and are available to the public.

Technology The use of science to do practical things such as improve transport.

Towpath A path beside a canal or river.

Traders People who buy and sell goods.

Vehicles Machines in which people or goods are transported from one place to another.

Further information

Places to visit:

Coventry Transport Museum (www.transport-museum.com)
The birthplace of the cycle and motor industry has Britain's largest museum collection of road transport.

Other transport museums include:
The National Railway Museum, York (www.nrm.org.uk)
London Transport Museum (www.ltmuseum.co.uk)
Grampian Transport Museum (www.gtm.org.uk)
South Yorkshire Aircraft Museum (www.aeroventure.org.uk)
The National Cycle Collection, Powys (www.cyclemuseum.org.uk)
Streetlife Museum, Hull

Websites:

For old images of transport you can search the picture galleries on the following websites:
www.picturethepast.org.uk
www.maryevans.com

www.ngfl-cymru.org.uk
looks at different types of transport through the ages and contains interactive activities and quizzes

Books to read:

Travel Through Time series, Jane Shuter, 2004 (Raintree)
Where You Live: Getting About, Ruth Nason, 2007 (Franklin Watts)
Journeys (What Was It Like in the Past?), Mandy Ross, 2003 (Heinemann)
Victorian Transport: The History Detective Investigates, Colin Stott, 2004 (Wayland)

Index

aeroplanes 7, 25-27
airports 26-27

barges 20-21
bicycles 8-9, 19
bridleways 11
buses 18-19

cars 7-9, 12-13, 16-17
cruises 25

dual carriageways 15

ferries 25

hansom cabs 10
horse-drawn carriages 10,
    14
horses 6, 10-11, 16, 20
horses and carts 6, 10, 14,
    16, 20

lorries 6

motorcycles 18
motorways 15

public transport 18-19

roads 6-7, 9-11, 14-20

ships 24-25

taxis 10, 19
towpaths 20-21
traffic lights 16-17
trains 20, 22-23
trams 18-19
transporting goods 6, 10, 20,
    22

walking 8-9

How have things changed?

Travel

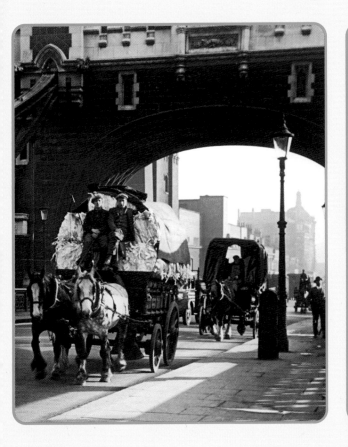

James Nixon

FRANKLIN WATTS

First published in 2008 by
Franklin Watts
338 Euston Road
London NW1 3BH

Franklin Watts Australia
Level 17/207 Kent Street
Sydney NSW 2000

ISBN: 978 0 7496 7844 9

Dewey classification number: 388

A CIP catalogue record for this book is available from the British Library.

Planning and production by Discovery Books Limited
Editor: James Nixon
Designer: Ian Winton

Photographs: p6 (top) Mary Evans Picture Library, p6 (bottom) Bobby Humphrey, p7 Chris Fairclough, p8 Mary Evans Picture Library, p9 (top) David Morgan/istockphoto.com, p9 (bottom) Chris Fairclough, p10 Ernest Ibbetson/Mary Evans Picture Library, p11 Chris Fairclough, p12 Getty Images, p13 Bobby Humphrey, p14 Stone Historical & Civic Society, p15 (top) Bobby Humphrey, p15 (bottom) Chris Fairclough, p16 Getty Images, p17 Bobby Humphrey, p18 Nottingham Historical Film Unit and www.picturethepast.org.uk, p19 (top) Chris Fairclough, p19 (middle) Bobby Humphrey, p19 (bottom) Chris Fairclough, p20 The Bromby Collection and www.picturethepast.org.uk, p21 Ann Taylor-Hughes/istockphoto.com, p22 J.H. Moss courtesy of Roger Carpenter, p23 Bobby Humphrey, p24 (top) Mary Evans Picture Library, p24 (bottom) J.H. Helsby/Getty Images, p25 istockphoto.com, p26 Mary Evans Picture Library, p27 (top) Liverpool John Lennon Airport, p27 (bottom) Roland Magunia/Getty Images.

Cover photos: (top) Nottingham Historical Film Unit and www.picturethepast.org.uk, (bottom) Bobby Humphrey.

Printed in China

Franklin Watts is a division of Hachette Children's Books, an Hachette Livre UK company
www.hachettelivre.co.uk